Quilt Notes

Candle mats offer a perfect opportunity for quilters to create small, quick projects. We use candles every day as well as for special occasions throughout the year. What better way for quilters to accent the beauty of their candles than with an irresistible quilted candle mat!

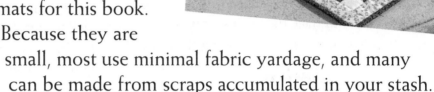

Ruth Swasey has created 20 attractive patterns for pieced candle mats for this book. Because they are small, most use minimal fabric yardage, and many can be made from scraps accumulated in your stash.

Enjoy making these small but creative pieced and quilted projects. You'll want to make a variety for use and enjoyment in your own home, but you'll also enjoy the speed with which you can create candle mats for giving.

Meet the Designer

Ruth M. Swasey has been making and designing quilts for more than 25 years. She enjoys manipulating designs and using lots of different fabrics in one quilt. Scrap quilts are her favorites. She sews most of her quilts by machine these days, but her first love is hand-piecing and -quilting, and she manages to have a few of those projects in her sewing basket.

As the first editor of Stitch 'N Sew Quilts and, later assistant editor of Quick & Easy Quilting and Quilt World, all published by House of White Birches, Ruth has been involved with quilting in the world of publishing since 1972. She has designed and stitched quilts for publication since that time.

As the mother of three children, Ruth has a busy life and still manages to keep quilting and sharing her designs with others.

General Instructions

Cutting & Piecing

Many of the pieces for the candle mats in this book may be quick-cut using a quilter's acrylic ruler and a rotary cutter. Others have irregular shapes and will require templates. Trace the template shapes on clear plastic template material and cut out on traced lines.

Some pieces have a mirror image and need to be reversed when cutting. Instructions will be given for the number of pieces to be cut with the traced template. You will then be instructed to reverse (turn over) the template to trace the reversed pieces.

Follow pattern instructions for assembling the blocks.

Marking

Any quilting designs should be marked on the quilt top before it is layered with backing and batting. A sharp, medium-lead pencil may be used on light background fabrics. Test the pencil marks to be sure they will wash out when quilting is complete, or be sure that your quilting stitches cover the line. Mechanical pencils with very fine points may also be used successfully to mark quilts.

Whatever marking tool you use should never show on the finished quilt.

Most of the designs in this book are quilted in the ditch and will require no marking.

Layering

Backing fabric and batting are usually cut slightly larger than the quilt top. The Fabric & Batting list will give suggested sizes for each project.

Place the backing wrong side up on a flat work surface. Place the batting on the backing and smooth it carefully. Place the pieced top on the batting and carefully smooth.

To hold the layers together for quilting, baste by hand or use safety pins. Safety pins work especially well for machine quilting.

Quilting may be done by hand or by machine in the design of your choice.

Binding

Trim the backing and batting layers flush with the top of the candle mat.

Double-fold, straight-grain binding may be successfully used on most of the small projects in this book.

Cut the selected fabric in 1½"-wide strips on the straight grain of the fabric. Join the strips as shown in Figure 1 to make binding of sufficient length.

Fold the binding lengthwise, wrong sides facing, and press.

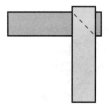

Figure 1
Join binding strips in a diagonal
seam as shown.

Several quilts in this book have curved edges and bias binding is recommended. Make the binding the same as above, but cut the 1½"-wide strips on the bias instead of on the straight grain.

Pin the folded binding along one edge of the quilt, starting in the middle of one side and aligning the raw edges. Stitch, with a walking foot if you have one, to within ¼" of the first corner; backstitch.

Turn the quilt; fold the binding at a 45-degree angle up and away from the quilt as shown in Figure 2.

Fold the binding back down, flush with the raw edge of the quilt as shown in Figure 3. Repeat at each corner as you stitch around the quilt.

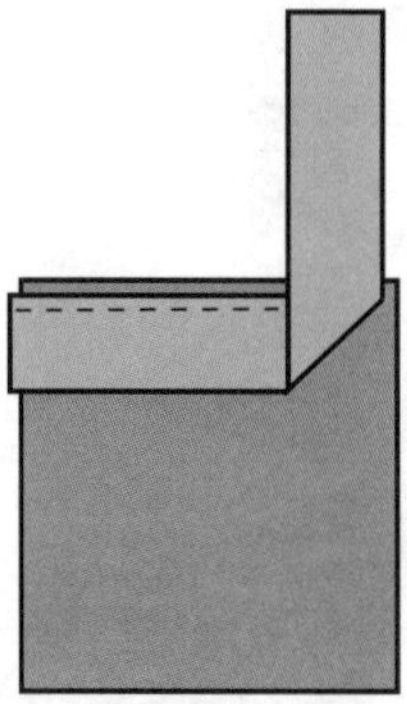

Figure 2
Fold binding at a 45-degree angle up and away from quilt.

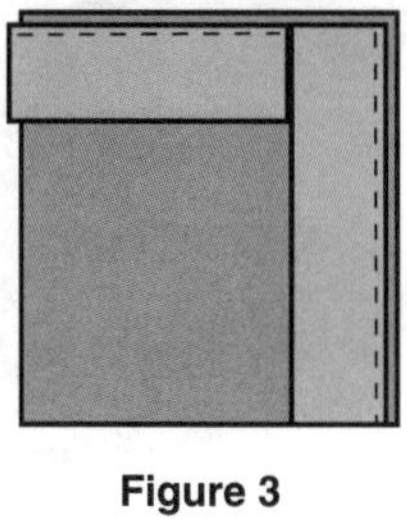

Figure 3
Fold binding back down flush with raw edge of quilt.

As you approach the beginning of the binding strip, stop stitching and overlap the binding ½" from the edge; trim. Join the two ends with a ¼" seam allowance and press the seam open. Reposition the joined binding along the edge of the quilt and resume stitching to the beginning.

To finish, bring the folded edge of the binding over the raw edges of the quilt and blind-stitch the folded edge of the binding in place over the machine-stitching line of the backside. ❖

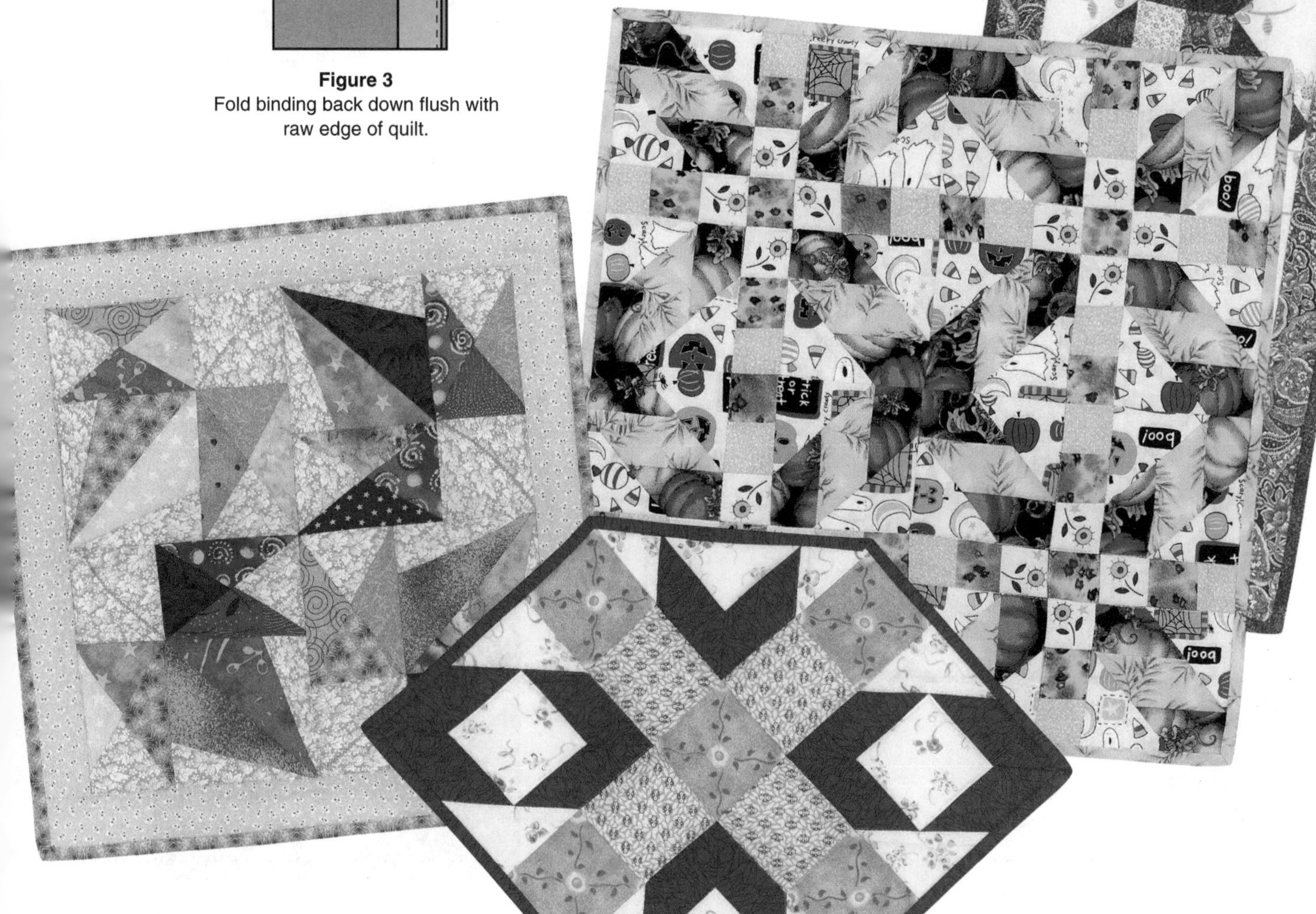

Friendship Circle

A patriotic theme appeals to everyone and fits any decor!

Project Specifications

Skill Level: Beginner
Candle Mat Size: 8½" x 8½"
Block Size: 6" x 6"

Fabric & Batting

- ¼ yard patriotic novelty print for piecing and binding
- Scraps of navy print
- Scraps of white print
- 2 squares red print 5⅛" x 5⅛"
- Backing 11" x 11"
- Thin batting 11" x 11"

Supplies & Tools

- Rotary-cutting tools
- All-purpose thread to blend with fabrics
- Red quilting thread

triangles to each side of block as shown in Placement Diagram.

4. Prepare for quilting as shown in General Instructions. Quilt as desired by hand or machine.

5. From patriotic novelty print cut and piece enough 1½"-wide strips to make 42" of binding as shown in General Instructions. Bind candle mat to finish. ❖

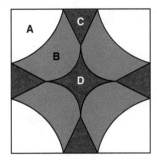

Friendship Circle
6" x 6" Block

Instructions

1. Trace and cut fabrics as instructed on templates.
2. Refer to 6" block drawing and piece by hand or machine.
3. Cut the two red print 5⅛" squares in half diagonally. Sew the long side of resulting

Friendship Circle
Placement Diagram
8½" x 8½"

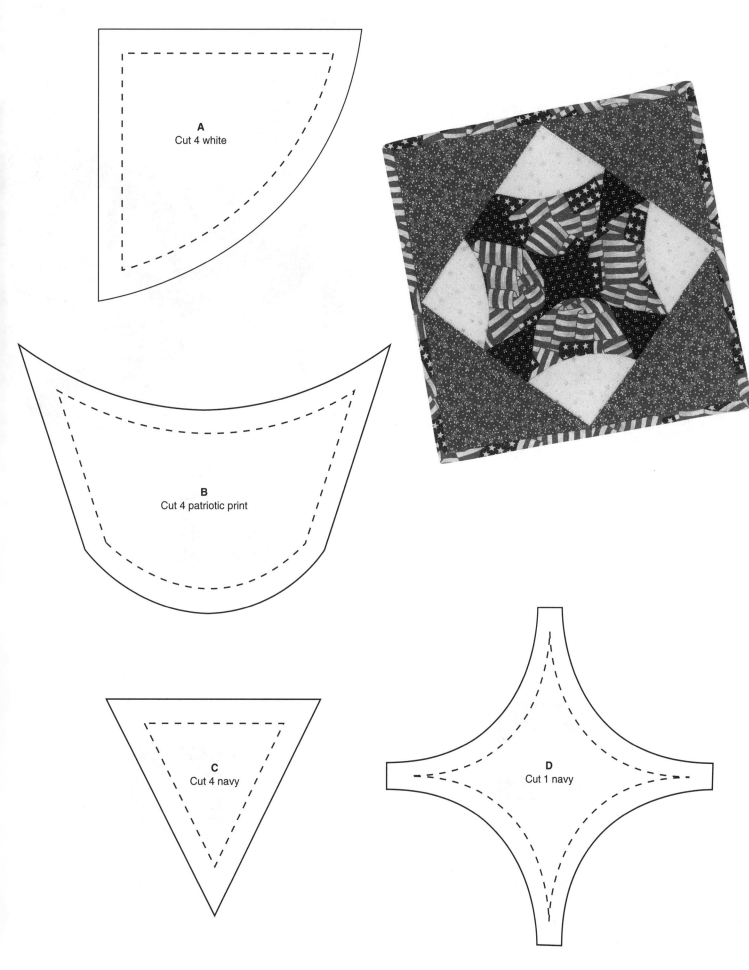

A
Cut 4 white

B
Cut 4 patriotic print

C
Cut 4 navy

D
Cut 1 navy

Daffodil Squares

Nothing says "Spring" like nodding golden daffodils.

Project Specifications
Skill Level: Beginner
Candle Mat Size: 16" x 16"

Fabric & Batting
- ¼ yard light background print
- ¼ yard daffodil print
- ¼ yard dark green print
- Backing 20" x 20"
- Thin batting 20" x 20"

Supplies & Tools
- Rotary-cutting tools
- All-purpose thread to blend with fabrics
- White quilting thread

Instructions

1. From daffodil print, cut nine B squares 2⅞" x 2⅞". From dark green print, cut 10 squares 2⅞" x 2⅞". Cut the dark green print squares in half diagonally for 20 A triangles. Sew four A triangles to the sides of five B squares as shown in Figure 1.

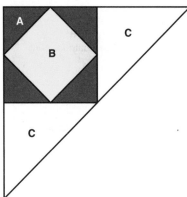

Figure 2
Sew two C triangles to 2 sides of 4 A/B units.

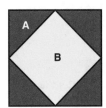

Figure 1
Sew A triangles to B squares as shown.

2. From light background fabric, cut four squares 4⅞" x 4⅞". Cut each in half diagonally to make eight C triangles. Sew one C triangle to two sides of each unit made in step 1 as shown in Figure 2 to complete four corner units.

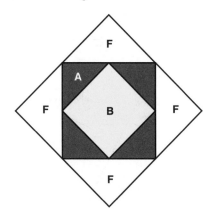

Figure 3
Sew one F triangle to each side of remaining A/B unit.

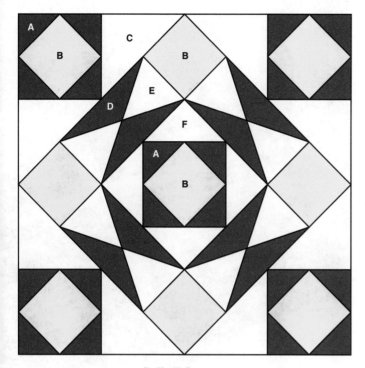

Daffodil Squares
Placement Diagram
16" x 16"

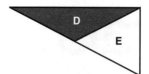

Figure 4
Join D and E as shown.

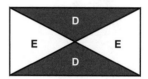

Figure 5
Join D/E units as shown.

5. Sew a daffodil square to each end of two D/E rectangles. Sew two D/E rectangles to each side of center square made in step 3. Sew together in rows as shown in Figure 6. Add one corner unit made in step 2 to complete the square as shown in Placement Diagram.

Figure 6
Sew rows together as shown.

3. From light background fabric, cut two squares 3¾" x 3¾". Cut each in half diagonally to make four F triangles. Sew one F triangle to each side of remaining unit made in step 1 as shown in Figure 3 to complete the center square.

4. From light background fabric, cut eight triangles with template E. From dark green print, cut eight triangles with template D. Sew one of each together as shown in Figure 4. Repeat for eight units. Join two units as shown in Figure 5. Repeat for four rectangles.

6. Prepare for quilting as shown in General Instructions. Quilt as desired by hand or machine.

7. From daffodil print, cut and piece enough 1½"-wide strips to make 2 yards of binding as shown in General Instructions. Bind candle mat to finish. ❖

E
Cut 8 light background print

D
Cut 8 dark green print

Garden Pathways

Flowers and vegetables blend perfectly in the garden!

Project Specifications

Skill Level: Beginner
Candle Mat Size: 18" x 18"
Block Size: 9" x 9"

Fabric & Batting

- ⅛ yard medium green print
- ¼ yard small pink print on dark green background
- ¼ yard medium pink flower print on dark background
- ½ yard medium pink print on yellow background
- Backing 22" x 22"
- Thin batting 22" x 22"

Supplies & Tools

- Rotary-cutting tools
- All-purpose thread to blend with fabrics
- Natural quilting thread

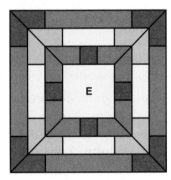

Garden Pathways
9" x 9" Block

Instructions

1. Use A template to cut 16 each medium pink flower print on dark background, medium green print, and small pink print on dark green background.

Reverse template to AR and cut the same number of the same templates reversed.

2. From medium pink flower print on dark background, cut 16 rectangles 1½" x 5½" for B. From medium pink print on yellow background, cut 16 rectangles 1½" x 3½" for C and four squares 3½" x 3½" for E. From small pink print on dark green background, cut 16 squares 1½" x 1½".

3. Sew A and AR (medium pink flower print on dark background) to each D as shown in Figure 1.

Figure 1
Sew A & AR to each side of D.

4. Sew A and AR (medium green print) to each C piece as shown in Figure 2.

Figure 2
Sew A & AR to each side of C.

5. Sew A and AR (small pink print on dark green background) to each B piece as shown in Figure 3.

Figure 3
Sew A & AR to each side of B.

6. Join the strips made in steps 2–4 into one unit as shown in Figure 4. Sew one unit to each side of each E piece to make one Garden Pathways block. Repeat for four blocks.

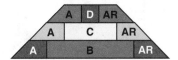

Figure 4
Join strips as shown.

7. Join four blocks as shown in Placement Diagram.

8. Prepare for quilting as shown in General Instructions. Quilt as desired by hand or machine.

9. From medium pink print on yellow background, cut and piece enough 1½"-wide strips to make 2¼ yards of binding as shown in General Instructions. Bind candle mat to finish. ❖

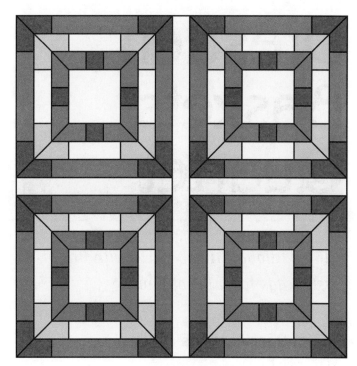

Garden Pathways
Placement Diagram
18" x 18"

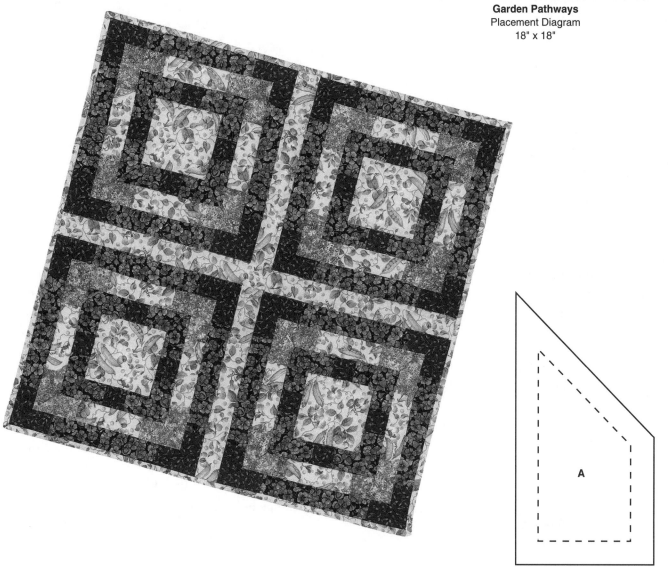

Dresden Baskets Quartet

Fill traditional little baskets with bright Easter eggs for a bit of whimsy.

Project Specifications

Skill Level: Beginner

Candle Mat Size: 26" x 8"

Block Size: 6" x 6"

Fabric & Batting

- ⅛ yard lavender print
- ¼ yard rose mottled
- ¼ yard paisley for borders and piecing
- ¼ yard light background print
- Scraps of bright prints for Easter eggs
- Backing 30" x 12"
- Thin batting 30" x 12"

Supplies & Tools

- Rotary-cutting tools
- All-purpose thread to blend with fabrics
- Scraps of fusible web
- Natural quilting thread

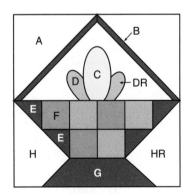

Dresden Basket
6" x 6" Block

Instructions

1. From light background print, cut four A rectangles 3½" x 6½". Trace template H and cut four pieces. Reverse template and cut four HR pieces.

2. From paisley, cut two strips each 1½" x 8½" and 1½" x 24½". Put aside for borders.

3. Each basket is pieced from a variety of triangles and squares using rose mottled, paisley and lavender print. Refer to the photo for ideas and cut 24 F squares 1½" x 1½". Cut eight squares 1⅞" x 1⅞". Cut the 1⅞" squares in half diagonally for 16 E triangles.

4. With template G, cut two pieces each from rose mottled and paisley.

5. On paper side of fusible web, trace four of each Easter egg shape (C, D and DR) and eight of basket handle B. Cut out each shape, leaving roughly ¼" margin around each traced line.

6. Following manufacturer's instructions, fuse egg shapes to selected bright print scraps and basket handles to rose mottled. Cut out on traced lines.

7. Arrange eggs and handles on A pieces, referring to Dresden Basket block drawing for placement; fuse. By hand or machine, work buttonhole or zigzag stitch around shapes.

8. On large work surface or design wall, arrange the pieces for four blocks. Refer to Placement Diagram for direction of baskets. When the arrangement of colors and fabrics pleases you, begin to piece one block.

9. Join four squares and add a triangle to each end as shown in Figure 1. Sew two squares together and add a triangle to each end as shown in Figure 2. Join the two rows.

Figure 1
Join squares and triangles as shown.

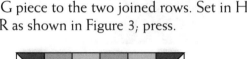

Figure 2
Join squares and triangles as shown.

10. Add a G piece to the two joined rows. Set in H and HR as shown in Figure 3; press.

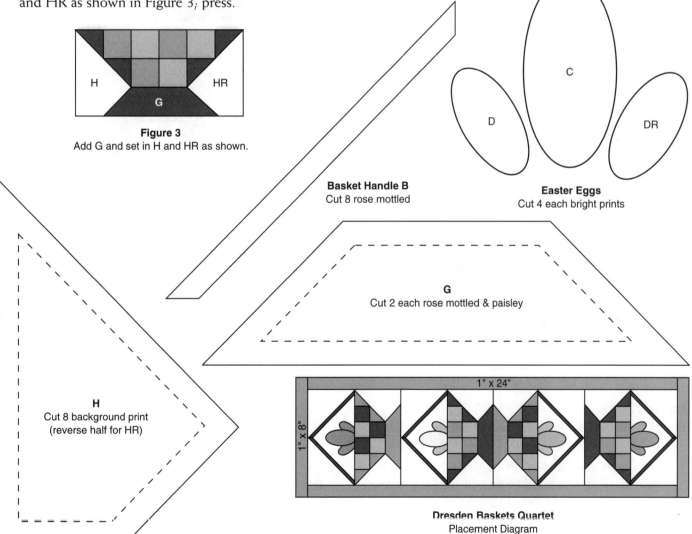

H   HR

G

Figure 3
Add G and set in H and HR as shown.

11. Sew basket half of block to appliquéd half to complete Dresden Basket block. Repeat for four blocks.

12. Sew four blocks together as shown in Placement Diagram. Sew long border strips, cut in step 2, to long edges of candle mat. Sew shorter strips to ends. Press seam allowances toward borders.

13. Prepare for quilting as shown in General Instructions. Quilt as desired by hand or machine.

14. From rose mottled, cut and piece enough 1½"-wide strips to make 2¼ yards of binding as shown in General Instructions. Bind candle mat to finish. ❖

C

D   DR

Easter Eggs
Cut 4 each bright prints

Basket Handle B
Cut 8 rose mottled

G
Cut 2 each rose mottled & paisley

H
Cut 8 background print
(reverse half for HR)

1" x 24"

1" x 8"

Dresden Baskets Quartet
Placement Diagram
26" x 8"

Twister Plus

Color and motion—the epitome of patchwork!

Project Specifications
Skill Level: Beginner
Candle Mat Size: 12" x 12"

Fabric & Batting
- ⅛ yard light background print
- ⅛ yard medium green print
- ⅛ yard green-and-purple print
- ¼ yard purple pansy print
- Backing 14" x 14"
- Thin batting 14" x 14"

Supplies & Tools
- Rotary-cutting tools
- All-purpose thread to blend with fabrics
- Natural quilting thread

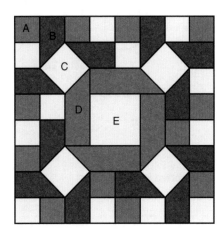

Twister Plus
12" x 12" Block

Instructions

Designer Note: *All seams should be sewn only to the end of the marked seam allowance to allow for smooth set-ins.*

1. From light background fabric, cut one E square 3½" x 3½". From purple pansy print, cut four pieces with template D. Sew D pieces to E as shown in Figure 1.

2. Cut 12 A squares each 2" x 2" from light

background print and medium green print. Sew one square of each color together for 12 sets.

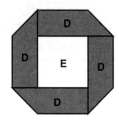

Figure 1
Sew D pieces to E as shown.

3. From green-and-purple print, cut 12 pieces with template B. From light background print, cut four C squares 2⅝" x 2⅝". Sew a B to three sides of C as shown in Figure 2. Repeat for four corner units.

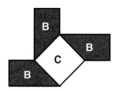

Figure 2
Sew a B to three sides of C.

4. Arrange the center, sewn in step 1, on a flat work surface. Place a unit sewn in step 3 at each corner with the C square aligned with the slanted edge of a D strip.

5. Checking the Placement Diagram carefully for color direction, position the sets of squares sewn in step 2 appropriately. Set in and sew.

6. Prepare for quilting as shown in General Instructions. Quilt as desired by hand or machine.

7. From purple pansy print, cut and piece enough 1½"-wide strips to make 2 yards of binding as shown in General Instructions. Bind candle mat to finish. ❖

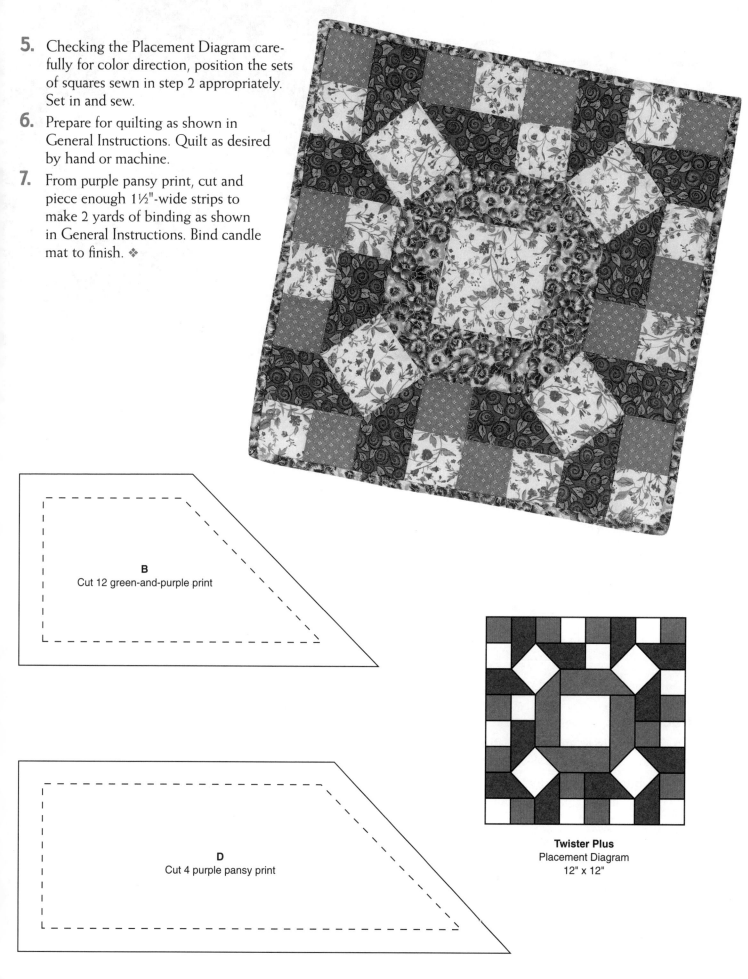

B
Cut 12 green-and-purple print

D
Cut 4 purple pansy print

Twister Plus
Placement Diagram
12" x 12"

Peek-a-Boo Squares

Bright, happy and delightfully scrappy!

Project Specifications

Skill Level: Beginner

Candle Mat Size: 11" x 11"

Block Size: 3" x 3"

Fabric & Batting

- ⅛ yard white-on-white print
- ⅛ yard bright stripe
- ¼ yard coordinating bright floral
- Backing 13" x 13"
- Thin batting 13" x 13"

Supplies & Tools

- Rotary-cutting tools
- All-purpose thread to blend with fabrics
- White quilting thread

Peek-a-Boo
3" x 3" Block

Instructions

1. From bright stripe and coordinating bright floral, cut 18 rectangles each 1½" x 2½".

2. From white-on-white print, cut two strips each 1½" x 9½" and 1½" x 11½". Put aside for borders. Cut nine squares 1½" x 1½".

3. Sew one bright striped strip to one white square as shown in Figure 1. Do not sew into the seam allowance. Continue to add strips in a counterclockwise direction, referring to block drawing for color sequence. Repeat for nine blocks.

Figure 1
Sew strip to square as shown.

4. Arrange blocks on work surface, referring to Placement Diagram for correct block rotation.

5. Sew blocks into rows of three each. Sew rows together.

6. Sew shorter border strips, cut in step 2, to two opposite sides of candle mat. Sew longer strips to top and bottom. Press seam allowances away from borders.

7. Prepare for quilting as shown in General Instructions. Quilt as desired by hand or machine.

8. From white-on-white print, cut and piece enough 1½"-wide strips to make 1½ yards of binding as shown in General Instructions. Bind candle mat to finish. ❖

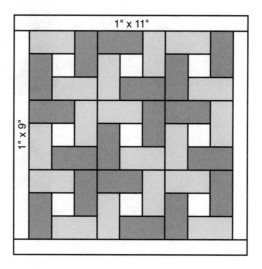

Peek-a-Boo Squares
Placement Diagram
11" x 11"

Jewel Star

Great optical illusions in this candle mat—curved as it looks, every seam is straight!

Project Specifications

Skill Level: Beginner
Candle Mat Size: 18" x 18
Block Size: 8" x 8"

Fabric & Batting

- ¼ yard light background print for piecing and borders
- ¼ yard light green print for piecing and binding
- ¼ yard yellow solid
- ¼ yard purple-and-teal print
- Backing 22" x 22"
- Thin batting 22" x 22"

Supplies & Tools

- Rotary-cutting tools
- All-purpose thread to blend with fabrics
- White quilting thread

AR. Repeat with appropriate color placement for four triangles. Sew triangles together for one block. Repeat for four blocks.

4. Arrange four blocks, referring to Placement Diagram for appropriate rotation.

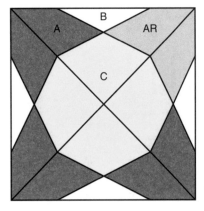

Jewel Star
8" x 8" Block

Instructions

1. From light background print, cut two strips each 1½" x 16½" and 1½" x 18½" for borders. Set aside.

2. Trace and cut pieces as instructed on templates.

3. Referring to block drawing for color placement, sew an A piece to a C piece and a B piece to an

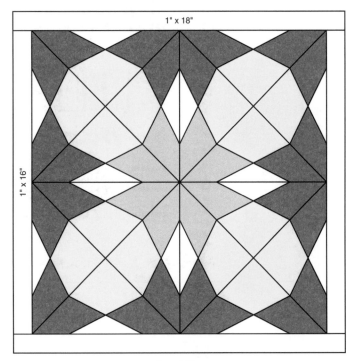

Jewel Star
Placement Diagram
18" x 18"

5. Sew two blocks in two rows. Sew rows together.

6. Sew two shorter strips cut in step 1 to opposite sides of mat. Sew two longer strips to top and bottom.

7. Prepare for quilting as shown in General Instructions. Quilt as desired by hand or machine.

8. From light background fabric, cut and piece enough 1½"-wide strips to make 2⅓ yards of binding as shown in General Instructions. Bind candle mat to finish. ❖

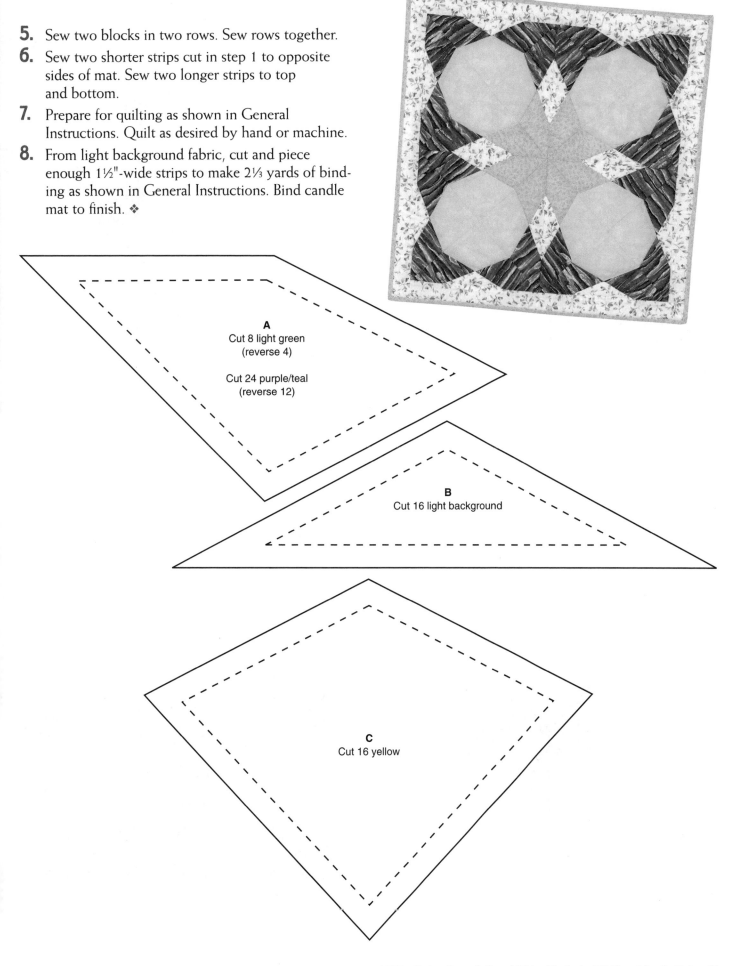

A
Cut 8 light green
(reverse 4)

Cut 24 purple/teal
(reverse 12)

B
Cut 16 light background

C
Cut 16 yellow

Floral Bouquet

Place this mat on-point for the best presentation of a bright bouquet.

Project Specifications

Skill Level: Intermediate
Candle Mat Size: 13" x 13"
Block Size: 4" x 4"

Fabric & Batting

- ⅛ yard yellow mottled
- ⅛ yard light floral print for borders
- ⅛ yard of pink-and-green floral print
- Scraps of medium green floral print
- Scraps of 3 different, but coordinating bright pinks
- ¼ yard of one coordinating bright pink for piecing and binding
- Backing 15" x 15"
- Thin batting 15" x 15"

Supplies & Tools

- Rotary-cutting tools
- All-purpose thread to blend with fabrics
- 1 spool white quilting thread

pieces. Reverse template and cut four of each fabric reversed.

2. From yellow mottled, cut 16 squares using A template.

3. From pink-and-green floral print, cut 16 triangles using B template.

4. Construct one star block from each pink print. Sew four C/CR units as shown in Figure 1. Join the units as shown in Figure 2. Set in the yellow corner A squares and pink-and-green floral B triangles. Repeat for four blocks and sew together as shown in Figure 3.

Figure 1
Join C/CR pieces.

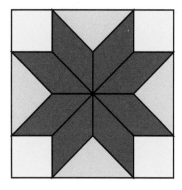

Star
4" x 4" Block

Instructions

1. From each of the bright pink fabrics, cut four C

Figure 2
Join C/CR units.

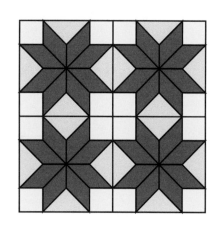

Figure 3
Join stars as shown.

5. Use template D to cut one medium green floral print and one pink-and-green floral print. Reverse the template and cut one more of each fabric. Join the triangles as shown in Figure 4. Note color placement.

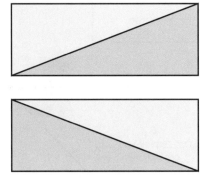

Figure 4
Join triangles as shown, noting color placement.

6. Cut one square each 3½" x 3½" from medium green floral print and pink-and-green floral print. Cut each in half diagonally. Join one floral and one green triangle as shown in Figure 5. Discard the other two triangles.

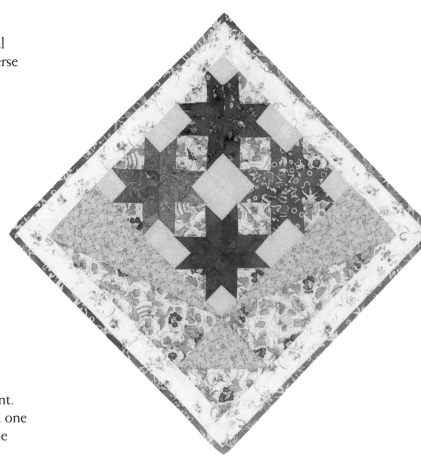

Floral Bouquet
Placement Diagram
13" x 13"

Figure 5
Join triangles as shown.

7. Refer to Placement Diagram and arrange units, carefully noting color placement. Join units in rows; join rows.

8. From light floral print, cut two strips each 1½" x 11½" and 1½" x 13½". Sew shorter strips to two opposite sides of candle mat. Sew longer strips to remaining two sides. Press seam allowances away from borders.

9. Prepare for quilting as shown in General Instructions. Quilt as desired by hand or machine.

10. From bright pink binding fabric, cut and piece enough 1½"-wide strips to make 1¾ yards of binding as shown in General Instructions. Bind candle mat to finish. ❖

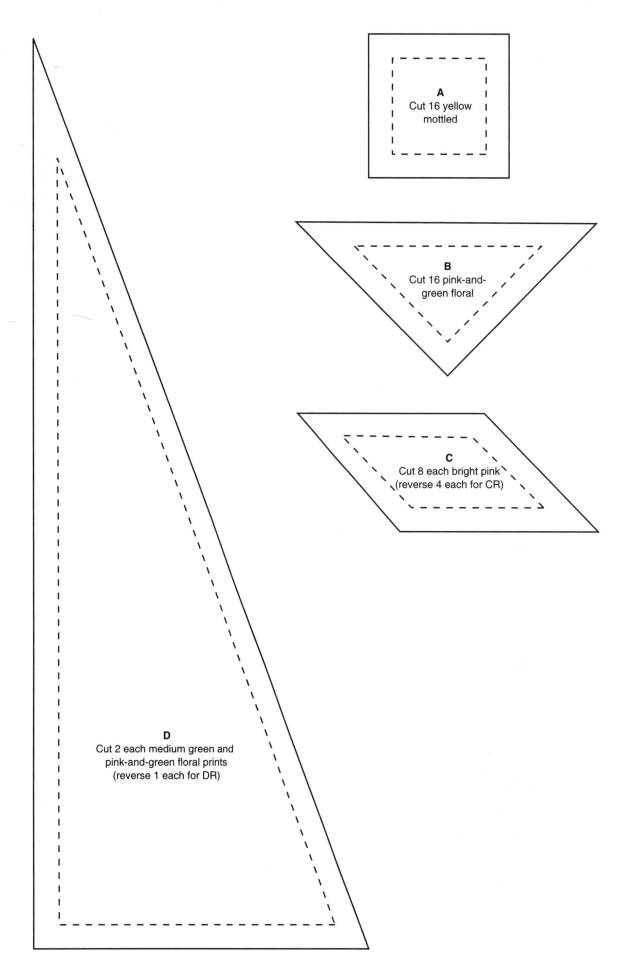

A
Cut 16 yellow
mottled

B
Cut 16 pink-and-
green floral

C
Cut 8 each bright pink
(reverse 4 each for CR)

D
Cut 2 each medium green and
pink-and-green floral prints
(reverse 1 each for DR)

Floral View

Soft curves seem to enhance the muted floral prints in this candle mat.

Project Specifications
Skill Level: Beginner
Candle Mat Size: 16½" x 10½"

Fabric & Batting
- ⅛ yard green vine print on neutral background
- ⅛ yard rose-and-green floral print
- ⅛ yard daisy print on green background
- ¼ yard green print
- Light neutral background print
- Backing 20" x 14"
- Thin batting 20" x 14"

Supplies & Tools
- Rotary-cutting tools
- All-purpose thread to blend with fabrics
- White quilting thread

Instructions

1. From rose-and-green floral print, cut eight E shapes. From light neutral background print, cut eight D shapes. Carefully pin and sew one of each shape together, easing along the curve. Make eight units.

2. From light neutral background print and daisy print, cut two squares each 3⅛" x 3⅛". Cut each square on the diagonal and stitch one triangle of each color together to make four half-square triangles.

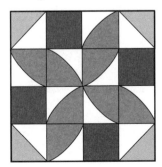

Figure 1
Arrange and sew squares as shown.

3. From green print, cut four squares 2¾" x 2¾".

4. Arrange all squares made in steps 1–3 on work surface or design wall as shown in Figure 1. Sew squares into rows and then join rows.

5. From rose-and-green floral print, cut four A shapes and two B shapes. Reverse B template and cut two more shapes.

6. From light neutral background print, cut two C shapes. Reverse template and cut two more shapes.

7. Carefully pin and sew B and C together, easing along the curve. Make four units. Join A and B/C units to make strip shown in Figure 2. Repeat for second strip.

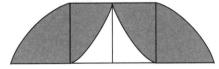

Figure 2
Sew strip as shown.

8. From green vine print on neutral background, cut two strips each 1¼" x 9½" and 1¼" x 11". Sew shorter strips to opposite sides of square constructed in step 4. Sew longer strips to top and bottom.

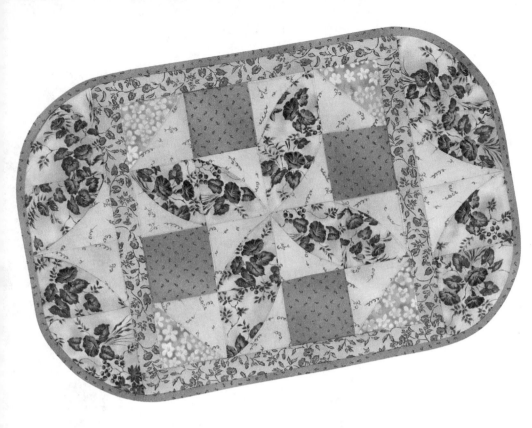

9. Add strips constructed in step 7 to each side of square as shown in Placement Diagram.

10. Prepare for quilting as shown in General Instructions. Quilt as desired by hand or machine.

11. From green print, cut and piece enough 1½"-wide strips to make 1¾ yards of bias binding as shown in General Instructions. Bias binding will ease better on the curves of this piece. Bind candle mat to finish. ❖

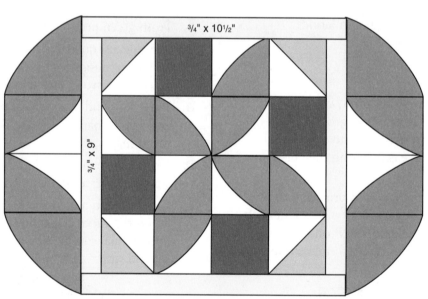

Floral View
Placement Diagram
16½" x 10½"

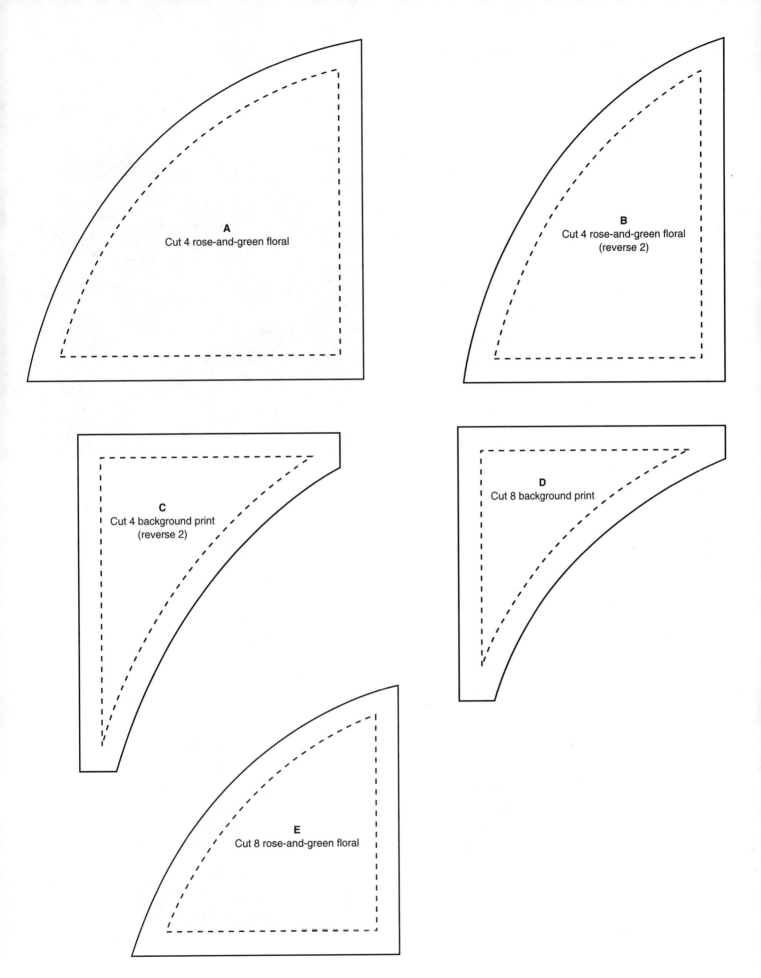

A
Cut 4 rose-and-green floral

B
Cut 4 rose-and-green floral
(reverse 2)

C
Cut 4 background print
(reverse 2)

D
Cut 8 background print

E
Cut 8 rose-and-green floral

Bright Star

This bright star will shine for any occasion when you substitute scraps of other themes and colors.

Project Specifications
Skill Level: Beginner
Candle Mat Size: 8" x 8"

Fabric & Batting
- ✄ Scraps of a bright print on green
- ✄ Scraps of turquoise, white, gold and red that coordinate with print
- ✄ 1⅛ yards purchased or self-made red binding
- ✄ Backing 10" x 10"
- ✄ Thin batting 10" x 10"

Supplies & Tools
- ✄ Rotary-cutting tools
- ✄ All-purpose thread to blend with fabrics
- ✄ White quilting thread

Instructions

1. From bright print on green, cut four shapes with template A. Cut one F square 2⅞" x 2⅞".

2. From white scraps, cut eight squares 1⅞" x 1⅞". Cut each in half for 16 B triangles.

3. From turquoise, cut eight squares 1½" x 1½" for C.

4. Sew two B shapes to each C as shown in Figure 1 for a total of eight units. Sew one B/C/B unit to each side of A units for a total of four squares as shown in Figure 2.

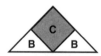

Figure 1
Sew 2 B shapes to C.

Figure 2
Sew 4 squares as shown.

5. From gold scraps, cut four D shapes. From red scraps, cut four squares 2¼" x 2¼". Cut each in half for eight E triangles.

6. Sew one E shape to two D shapes as shown in Figure 3 and Figure 4.

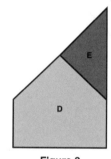

Figure 3
Sew 2 units as shown.

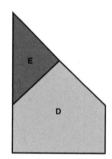

Figure 4
Sew 2 units as shown.

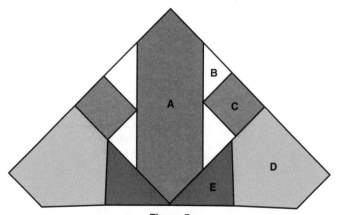

Figure 5
Sew D/E shapes to squares as shown.

7. Sew D/E shapes to two sides of A/B/C squares as shown in Figure 5.

8. Sew two E triangles to two opposite sides of F square (cut in step 1) as shown in Figure 6. Set in two remaining A/B/C squares as shown in Figure 7.

9. Sew units constructed in step 7 to each side of center strip as shown in Placement Diagram.

10. Prepare for quilting as shown in General Instructions. Quilt as desired by hand or machine.

11. Bind quilt with purchased or self-made red binding as shown in General Instructions. ❖

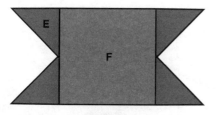

Figure 6
Sew E triangles to each side of F as shown.

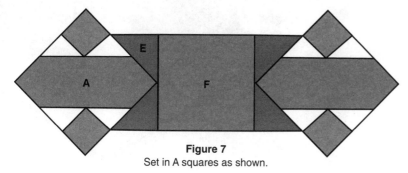

Figure 7
Set in A squares as shown.

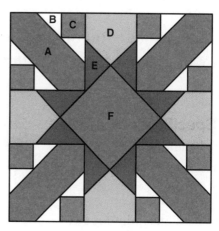

Bright Star
Placement Diagram
8" x 8"

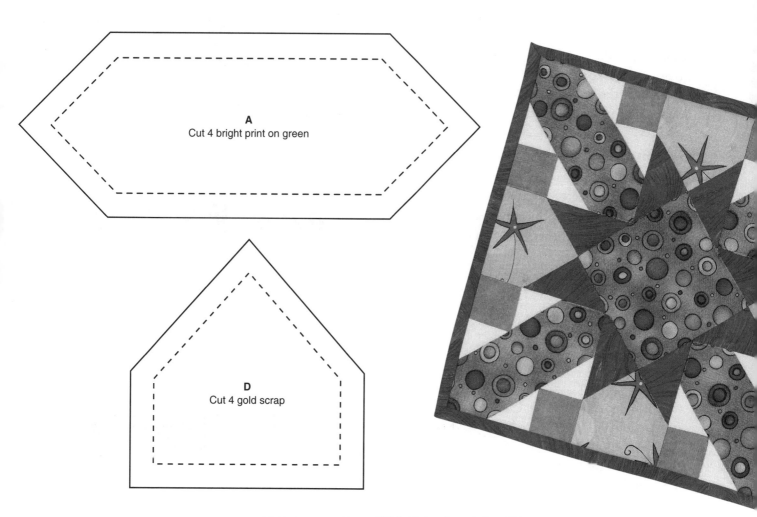

A
Cut 4 bright print on green

D
Cut 4 gold scrap

Blue & White Saw Blades

What could be more traditional than blue and white in this old favorite pattern?

Project Specifications
Skill Level: Beginner
Candle Mat Size: 15" x 15"

Fabric & Batting
- ½ yard dark blue print for piecing and binding
- ½ yard blue print on white background for piecing and borders
- ⅛ yard white-on-white print
- Backing 19" x 19"
- Thin batting 19" x 19"

Supplies & Tools
- Rotary-cutting tools
- All-purpose thread to match fabrics
- White quilting thread

Instructions

1. From dark blue print and blue print on white background, cut 36 squares each 1⅞" x 1⅞".

2. On backside of each light square mark a diagonal line from corner to corner as shown in Figure 1.

Figure 1
Draw a line corner to corner.

3. Layer one light square on one dark square. Sew ¼" each side of center line. Cut on center line to obtain two half-square triangles; press. Repeat for 72 half-square triangles.

4. Sew together three half-square triangles made in step 3 as shown in Figure 2. Repeat for 24 units.

Figure 2
Sew 3 squares as shown.

5. From white-on-white fabric, cut 16 squares 1½" x 1½". Join four white squares with three half-square triangle units as shown in Figure 3. Repeat for four strips.

Figure 3
Make 4 strips as shown.

6. From dark blue print, cut four squares 3½" x 3½". From blue print on white background, cut five squares 3½" x 3½".

7. Alternate half-square triangle units with 3½" squares as shown in Figure 4. Carefully note orientation of colors. Repeat for two strips.

Figure 4
Sew 2 strips as shown.

8. Sew one strip as shown in Figure 5.

Figure 5
Make 1 strip as shown.

9. Alternate strips with those made in step 5. Carefully check Placement Diagram for correct placement of strips and colors. Sew strips together.

10. From blue print on white background, cut two border strips each 1½" x 13½" and 1½" x 15½". Sew two shorter strips to two opposite sides of mat. Sew longer strips to top and bottom.

11. Prepare for quilting as shown in General Instructions. Quilt as desired by hand or machine.

12. From dark blue print, cut and piece enough 1½"-wide strips to make 2 yards of binding as shown in General Instructions. Bind candle mat to finish. ❖

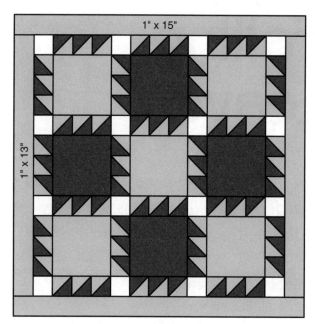

Blue & White Saw Blades
Placement Diagram
15" x 15"

Falling Leaves

Spicy cinnamon or candy apple would be perfect scents for candles to be used on this mat.

Project Specifications

Skill Level: Beginner
Candle Mat Size: 12" x 12"
Block Size: 5" x 5"

Fabric & Batting

- ¼ yard tan print for background
- ¼ yard orange print for piecing and binding
- ⅛ yard yellow print for borders
- Scraps of rust, orange, yellow and gold
- Backing 14" x 14"
- Thin batting 14" x 14"

Supplies & Tools

- Rotary-cutting tools
- All-purpose thread to match fabrics
- Natural quilting thread

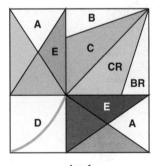

Leaf
5" x 5" Block

Instructions

1. From yellow print, cut two strips each 1½" x 10½" and 1½" x 12½". Put aside for borders.

2. From tan background print, cut eight A pieces. Use template B to cut four pieces. Reverse template and cut four more. Cut four D squares 2½" x 2½".

3. From a variety of rust, orange, yellow and gold scraps (including binding fabric), cut 8 A, 16 E and four C pieces. Reverse the C template and cut four C shapes reversed.

4. Referring to the block drawing, arrange pieces to achieve a pleasing color combination. Be careful to place background pieces in correct areas. Repeat for four blocks.

5. Sew A and E pieces as shown in Figure 1 (two units for each block). Sew B/C and BR/CR pieces as shown in Figure 2.

Figure 1
Sew A and E pieces as shown.

Figure 2
Sew B/C and BR/CR pieces as shown.

6. Referring to block drawing, join one A/E unit and the B/C/CR/BR unit for one row. Join a D square and the second A/E unit for the second row. Join rows to make one block. Repeat for four blocks.

7. Referring to block drawing, draw a stem on each leaf across the D square. With orange thread and narrow zigzag, stitch on the drawn line.

8. Referring to Placement Diagram, arrange blocks in two rows and sew.

9. Sew shorter strips cut in step 1 to opposite sides of quilt. Sew longer strips to top and bottom.

10. Prepare for quilting as shown in General Instructions. Quilt as desired by hand or machine.

11. From orange print, cut and piece enough 1½"-wide strips to make 1½ yards of binding as shown in General Instructions. Bind candle mat to finish. ❖

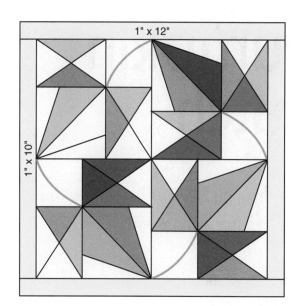

Falling Leaves
Placement Diagram
12" x 12"

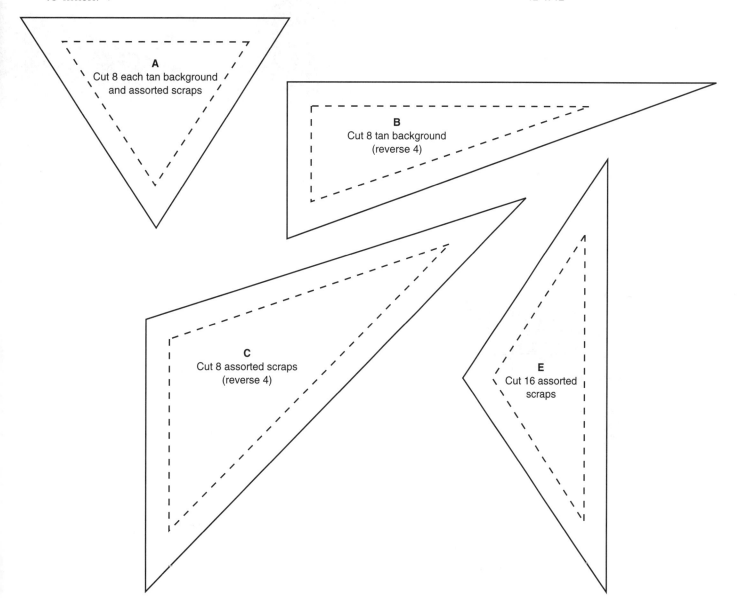

A
Cut 8 each tan background and assorted scraps

B
Cut 8 tan background
(reverse 4)

C
Cut 8 assorted scraps
(reverse 4)

E
Cut 16 assorted scraps

Pumpkin Patch

The whole jack-o'-lantern will want to rest on this festive candle mat.

Project Specifications
Skill Level: Beginner
Candle Mat Size: 14" x 14"
Block Size: 7" x 7"

Fabric & Batting
- ⅛ yard predominantly orange novelty print
- ⅛ yard light background novelty print
- ¼ yard lime green print
- Orange, yellow and light background scraps
- Backing 17" x 17"
- Thin batting 17" x 17"

Supplies & Tools
- Rotary-cutting tools
- All-purpose thread to blend with fabrics
- White quilting thread

Pumpkin Patch
7" x 7" Block

Instructions
1. Use template A to cut 32 shapes from predominantly orange novelty print. Use template B to cut16 shapes from lime green print.
2. From light background print, cut 16 squares 2⅞" x 2⅞". Cut each in half diagonally for 32 C triangles.
3. From variety of coordinating scraps, cut 52 squares 1½" x 1½".
4. Sew an A shape to each side of B as shown in Figure 1. Sew a C triangle to each side of unit as shown in Figure 2.

Figure 1
Sew an A shape to each side of B.

Figure 2
Sew a C triangle to each side of unit.

5. Sew three D squares together as shown in Figure 3. Repeat for eight sets. Sew seven D squares together as shown in Figure 4. Repeat for four sets.

Figure 3
Sew D squares together as shown.

Figure 4
Sew 7 squares as shown.

Pumpkin Patch
Placement Diagram
14" x 14"

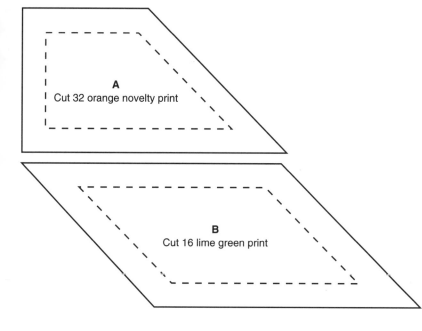

A
Cut 32 orange novelty print

B
Cut 16 lime green print

6. For one block, join two A/B/C units with one three-piece D unit as shown in Figure 5. Note rotation of squares. Repeat, again rotating squares, and join two rows with a strip of seven D squares as shown in Figure 6. Repeat for four blocks.

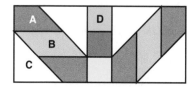

Figure 5
Join units as shown.

Figure 6
Join units as shown.

7. Referring to Placement Diagram, join blocks in two rows of two blocks each and sew together.

8. Prepare for quilting as shown in General Instructions. Quilt as desired by hand or machine.

9. From lime green print, cut and piece enough 1½"-wide strips to make 2 yards of binding as shown in General Instructions. Bind candle mat to finish. ❖

Mantel Fans

Choose pastel reproduction prints for the soft 1930s look that we all love.

Project Specifications

Skill Level: Beginner
Candle Mat Size: 19" x 11"
Block Size: 4" x 4"

Fabric & Batting

- ⅛ yard blue reproduction print for borders
- ¼ yard green reproduction print for binding
- ¼ yard white background print (model has a narrow stripe)
- Variety of green and blue reproduction prints for fans
- Backing 22" x 14"
- Thin batting 22" x 14"

Supplies & Tools

- Rotary-cutting tools
- All-purpose thread to blend with fabrics
- White quilting thread

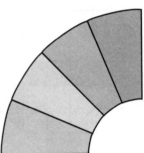

Figure 1
Sew 4 pieces together as shown.

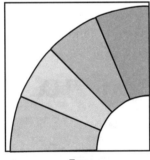

Fan
4" x 4" Block

Instructions

1. From white background print, cut eight squares 4½" x 4½".

2. Cut 16 A pieces each from blue and green reproduction prints.

3. Sew four blue A pieces together as shown in Figure 1. Repeat for four units. Repeat with green A pieces for four units.

4. Turn under the curved edges of each unit ¼". Referring to block drawing, appliqué each unit to a 4½" background square.

5. Referring to Placement Diagram, arrange appliquéd blocks on work surface in correct position. Sew blocks together in two rows of four blocks each. Sew the two rows together.

6. From blue reproduction print, cut two strips each 2" x 11½" and 2" x 16½". Sew the longer strips to the long edges of the mat. Sew the shorter strips to the remaining two sides.

7. Prepare for quilting as shown in General Instructions. Quilt as desired by hand or machine.

8. From green reproduction print, cut and piece enough 1½"-wide strips to make 2 yards of binding as shown in General Instructions. Bind candle mat to finish. ❖

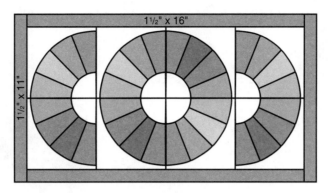

Mantel Fans
Placement Diagram
19" x 11"

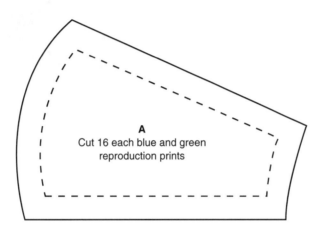

A
Cut 16 each blue and green
reproduction prints

Prickles

Add a spectacular pieced border to a floral print rectangle for a sumptuous design.

Project Specifications

Skill Level: Beginner
Candle Mat Size: 14" x 9"

Fabric & Batting

- ⅛ yard light green print
- ¼ yard dark green print
- ¼ yard floral print
- ¼ yard red batik for border and binding
- Backing 17" x 12"
- Thin batting 17" x 12"

Supplies & Tools

- Rotary-cutting tools
- All-purpose thread to blend with fabrics
- White quilting thread

Instructions

1. Using template A, cut 30 triangles from dark green print and 28 triangles from light green print.

2. Sew four light triangles and five dark triangles together as shown in Figure 1. Repeat for two strips.

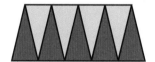

Figure 1
Sew triangles as shown.

3. Sew ten dark and nine light triangles together as in previous step, starting and ending with dark triangles. From floral print cut four pieces with template B. Sew one to each end of triangle strip. Repeat for two strips.

4. From floral print fabric, cut one rectangle 4½" x 9½" for center panel.

5. From red batik, cut two strips each 1" x 9½" and 1" x 5½". Sew longer strips to long sides of center panel and shorter strips to ends.

6. Sew the short strips made in step 2 to ends of panel. Sew long strips made in step 3 to sides of panel.

7. Prepare for quilting as shown in General Instructions. Quilt as desired by hand or machine.

8. From red batik, cut and piece enough 1½"-wide strips to make 1½ yards of binding as shown in General Instructions. Bind candle mat to finish. ❖

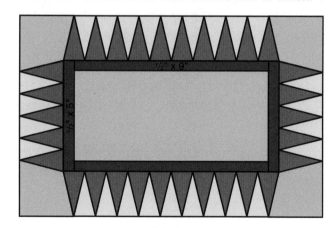

Prickles
Placement Diagram
14" x 9"

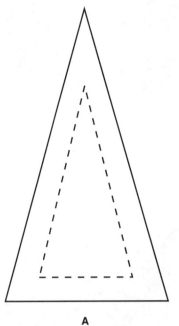

A
Cut 30 dark green print
and 28 light green print

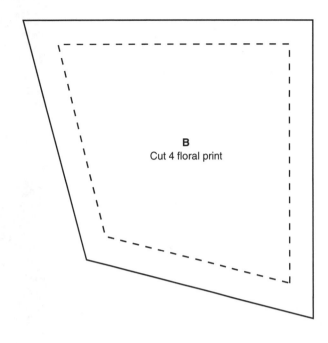

B
Cut 4 floral print

Egg-citing Ovals

Find a brilliant theme fabric and spin off some bright elliptical shapes for a mat with an impact!

Project Specifications
Skill Level: Beginner
Candle Mat Size 39" x 18"

Fabric & Batting
- ¼ yard bright teal fabric for binding and appliqué
- ⅓ yard bright novelty fabric
- Scraps of bright pink, orange and lime green
- ½ yard very lightly marbled background fabric
- Backing 43" x 43"
- Thin batting 43" x 43"

Supplies & Tools
- Rotary-cutting tools
- ½ yard fusible web
- Machine-embroidery threads to match bright scraps
- All-purpose thread to match fabrics
- White quilting thread

Instructions

1. From bright novelty print, cut two strips each 2" x 18½" and 2" x 36½". Put aside for borders.

2. Trace appliqué shapes on paper side of fusible web as directed on patterns. Cut out leaving roughly ¼" around traced shapes.

3. Following manufacturer's instructions, fuse to selected fabrics. Cut out on traced lines.

4. From lightly marbled background fabric, cut 36 rectangles 3½" x 5½".

5. Align novelty print shapes with long edges of 12 rectangles; fuse.

6. Center remaining shapes on remaining rectangles; fuse.

7. With machine-embroidery thread that matches each fabric, work narrow zigzag or satin stitch around each shape.

8. Refer to Placement Diagram for layout and arrange rectangles in rows. Stitch together in rows and then sew rows together.

9. Sew longer strips cut in step 1 to long sides of mat. Sew shorter strips to top and bottom.

10. Prepare for quilting as shown in General Instructions. Quilt as desired by hand or machine.

11. From bright teal, cut and piece enough 1½"-wide strips to make 3½ yards of binding as shown in General Instructions. Bind candle mat to finish. ❖

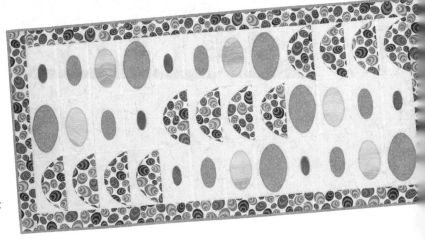

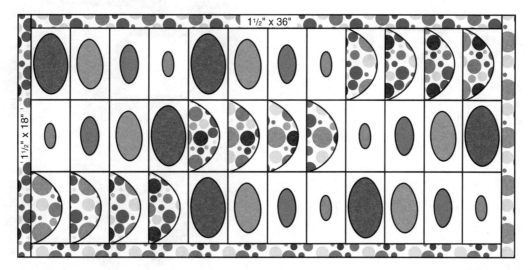

Egg-citing Ovals
Placement Diagram
39" x 18"

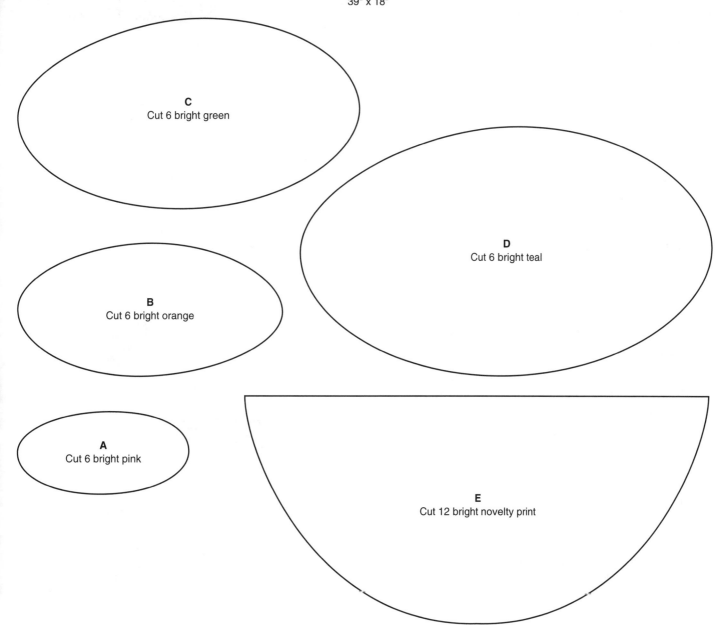

C
Cut 6 bright green

D
Cut 6 bright teal

B
Cut 6 bright orange

A
Cut 6 bright pink

E
Cut 12 bright novelty print

Hexagon Star

Not every candle mat is restricted to four sides! A change of shape contributes interest.

Project Specifications

Skill Level: Beginner

Candle Mat Size: Approximately 14" x 9"

Fabric & Batting

- ⅛ yard medium pink print
- ⅛ yard lighter pink print
- ⅛ yard light background print
- ¼ yard dark rose for piecing and binding
- Backing 17" x 12"
- Thin batting 17" x 12"

Supplies & Tools

- Rotary-cutting tools
- All-purpose thread to blend with fabrics
- White quilting thread

Instructions

1. With template A, cut six shapes from dark rose. Reverse the template and cut six additional shapes (AR).

2. From medium pink print, cut five B squares 2½" x 2½". From lighter pink print, cut four B squares 2½" x 2½".

3. From light background print, cut two B squares 2½" x 2½". Cut three squares 2⅞" x 2⅞". Cut in half diagonally for six C triangles. Cut two squares 2¼" x 2¼". Cut in half for four D triangles.

Figure 1
Join 5 squares as shown.

4. Sew three medium pink B squares together with two lighter pink B squares as shown in Figure 1. Sew one light pink square to one medium pink square for one unit. Repeat for two units.

5. Sew two A diamonds to one light background square as shown in Figure 2. Add two AR diamonds as shown in Figure 3.

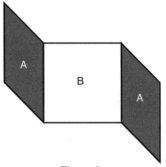

Figure 2
Sew A diamonds to square.

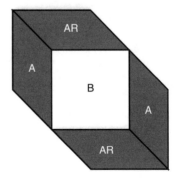

Figure 3
Add AR diamonds.

6. Add two C triangles as shown in Figure 4 to complete square. Repeat for two squares.

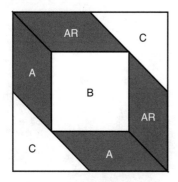

Figure 4
Add C triangles.

7. Sew an A and an AR diamond together and set in a C triangle as shown in Figure 5. Add a D triangle to each side as shown in Figure 6. Repeat for two triangles.

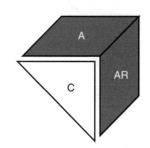

Figure 5
Sew A and AR together and set in C.

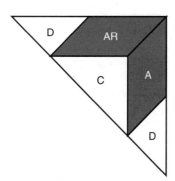

Figure 6
Add 2 D triangles.

8. Arrange all units as shown in Figure 7. Sew units together in rows and then join rows.

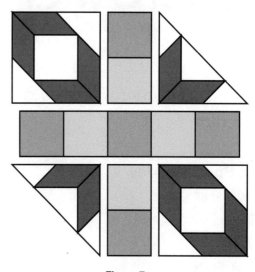

Figure 7
Arrange units as shown.

9. Prepare for quilting as shown in General Instructions. Quilt as desired by hand or machine.

10. From dark rose fabric, cut and piece enough 1½"-wide strips to make 1¼ yards of binding as shown in General Instructions. Bind candle mat to finish. ❖

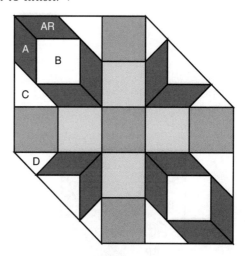

Hexagon Star
Placement Diagram
Aproximately 14" x 9"

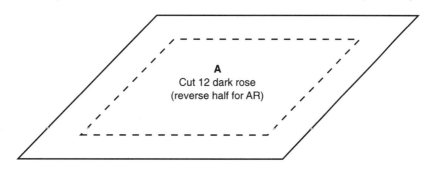

A
Cut 12 dark rose
(reverse half for AR)

Mayflower

The generous size of this mat makes it double as a table runner. It could easily be made even longer.

Project Specifications

Skill Level: Beginner
Candle Mat Size: 25" x 13"
Block Size: 5" x 5"

Fabric & Batting

- ⅛ yard yellow print
- ⅛ yard dark blue print
- ⅛ yard each of 2 different blue-on-white prints (blue 1 and blue 2)
- ¼ yard white-on-white print
- ½ yard medium blue floral print for piecing and binding
- Backing 29" x 17"
- Thin batting 29" x 17"

Supplies & Tools

- Rotary-cutting tools
- All-purpose thread to blend with fabrics
- White quilting thread

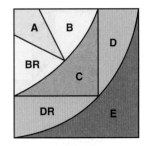

Mayflower
5" x 5" Block

Instructions

1. Use template A to cut eight shapes from yellow print. Use template B to cut six shapes from one blue-on-white print (blue 1) and two from the other blue-on-white print (blue 2). Reverse the B template and cut six blue 1 and two blue 2 BR shapes.

2. Sew one B and one BR to each yellow A as shown in Figure 1.

Figure 1
Sew B and BR to A.

3. Use template C to cut eight shapes from dark blue print. Sew one C to each B/A/BR unit as shown in Figure 2.

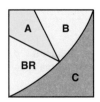

Figure 2
Add C as shown.

4. Use template D to cut eight shapes from blue-on-white print (blue 2). Reverse the D template and cut eight DR shapes from the same blue-on-white print. Sew one D and one DR to C as shown in Figure 3.

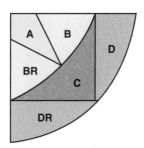

Figure 3
Sew D and DR to C.

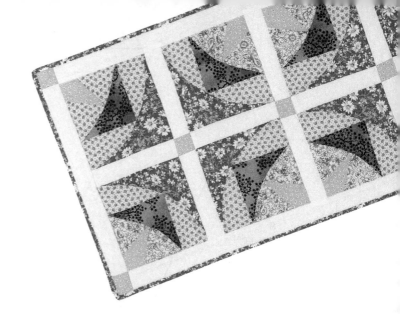

5. Use template E to cut eight shapes from medium blue floral print. Sew to pieced unit as shown in block diagram. Repeat for eight blocks.

6. From white-on-white print, cut two strips each 1½" x 11½" and 1½" x 23½". Put aside for borders. Cut 10 strips 1½" x 5½".

7. Place eight blocks on work surface, referring carefully to Placement Diagram for direction of each block.

8. Join each block in first row with block directly under it with one 1½" x 5½" strip.

Figure 4
Sew yellow square between 2 strips as shown.

9. From yellow print, cut seven 1½" x 1½" squares. Sew one yellow square between two white 1½" x 5½" strips as shown in Figure 4. Repeat for three units. Sew one unit between each pair of blocks as shown in Placement Diagram.

10. Sew longer border strips cut in step 6 to long sides of mat. Sew one yellow 1½" x 1½" square to each end of shorter border strips. Sew to ends of mat.

11. Prepare for quilting as shown in General Instructions. Quilt as desired by hand or machine.

12. From medium blue floral print, cut and piece enough 1½"-wide strips to make 2½ yards of binding as shown in General Instructions. Bind candle mat to finish. ❖

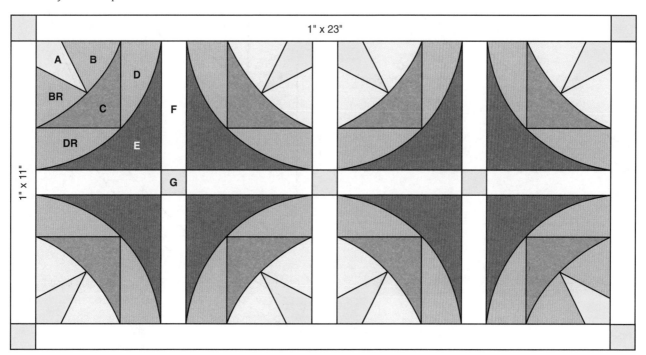

Mayflower
Placement Diagram
25" x 13"

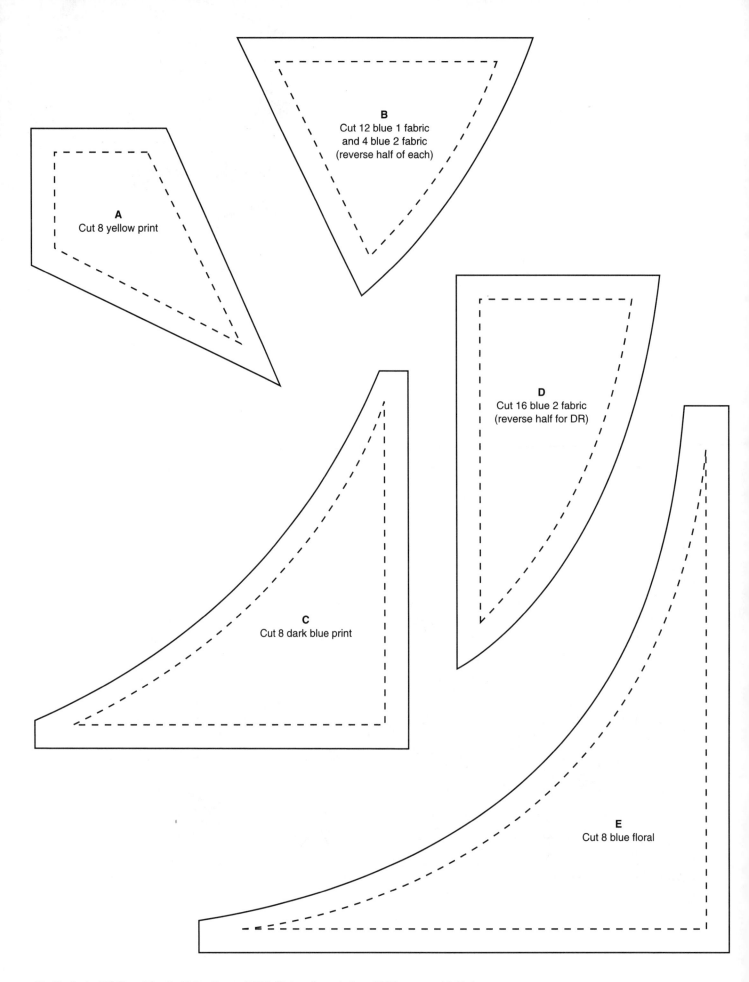

A
Cut 8 yellow print

B
Cut 12 blue 1 fabric
and 4 blue 2 fabric
(reverse half of each)

C
Cut 8 dark blue print

D
Cut 16 blue 2 fabric
(reverse half for DR)

E
Cut 8 blue floral

Easy Mariner's Compass

We often avoid this pattern because it is too challenging. Give this one a try. It works!

Project Specifications

Skill Level: Beginner
Candle Mat Size: 12" diameter
Compass Size: 10" diameter

Fabric & Batting

- ⅛ yard red mottled
- ⅛ yard white background
- ¼ yard green mottled
- ¼ yard red-and-green paisley for piecing and binding
- Backing 15" diameter circle
- Thin batting 15" diameter circle

Supplies & Tools

- Rotary-cutting tools
- All-purpose thread to blend with fabrics
- White quilting thread

Instructions

1. Use template C to cut four shapes from red-and-green paisley. Use template D to cut four shapes from white background. Reverse template and cut four DR from white background.

2. Sew one D and one DR to each C as shown in Figure 1. Make four units.

3. Use template B to cut four shapes from red mottled. Sew one B between each D/C/DR unit to form a circle as shown in block drawing. The compass will have a round opening in the center.

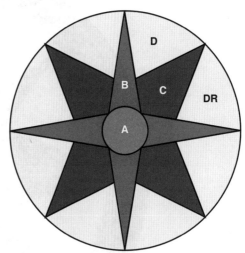

Mariner's Compass
10"-diameter Block

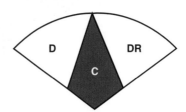

Figure 1
Sew D and DR to C as shown.

4. Press carefully. Use template A to cut one shape from green mottled. Appliqué A over opening in circle.

5. Use template E to cut four shapes from green mottled. Carefully, without stretching, sew E pieces to outer edges of circle. Align seams at the point of each B.

6. Prepare for quilting as shown in General Instructions. Quilt as desired by hand or machine.

7. From paisley, cut and piece enough 1½"-wide bias strips to make 1½ yards of bias binding as shown in General Instructions. Bias will be necessary to bind the compass curves. Bind candle mat to finish. ❖

Easy Mariner's Compass
Placement Diagram
12" diameter

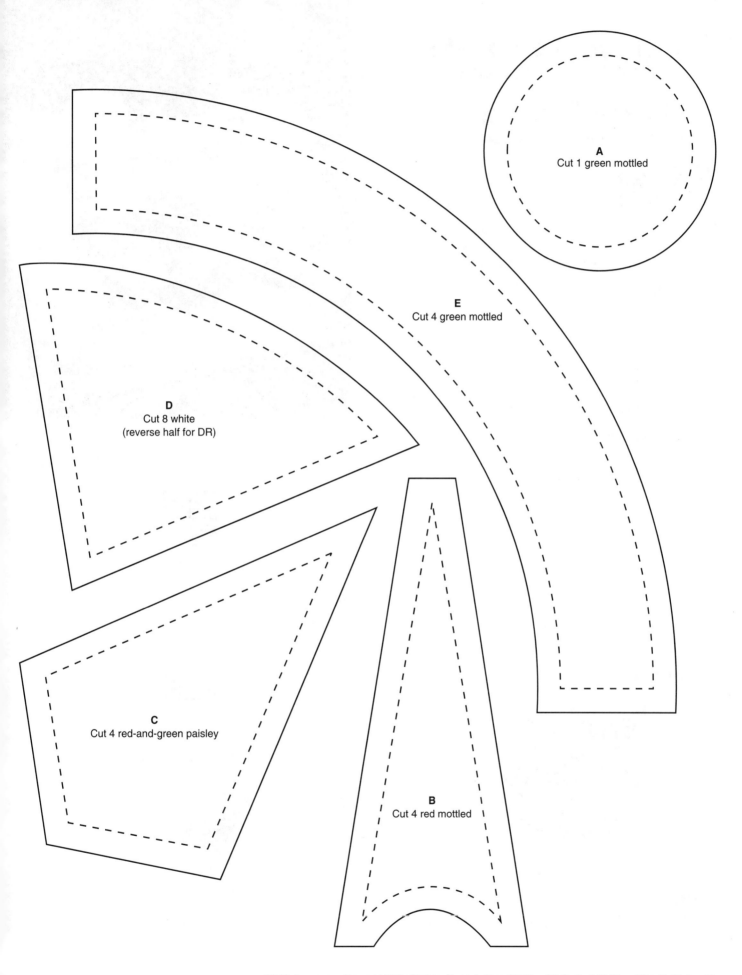

A
Cut 1 green mottled

E
Cut 4 green mottled

D
Cut 8 white
(reverse half for DR)

C
Cut 4 red-and-green paisley

B
Cut 4 red mottled

Four-Patch Christmas Star

Candles and Christmas go together naturally!

Project Specifications

Skill Level: Beginner
Candle Mat Size: 12" x 12"
Block Size: 9" x 9"

Fabric & Batting

- ⅛ yard white-on-white print fabric
- ⅛ yard red print fabric
- ⅛ yard Christmas print on white background for borders and piecing
- ¼ yard holly print fabric for piecing and binding
- Backing 14" x 14"
- Thin batting 14" x 14"

Supplies & Tools

- Rotary-cutting tools
- All-purpose thread to blend with fabrics
- White quilting thread

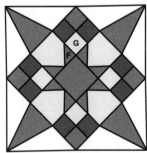

Four-Patch Christmas Star
9" x 9" Block

Instructions

1. From Christmas print on white background, cut four B strips 2" x 9½" for borders. Put aside.

2. Using squares cut from G template, sew four Four-Patch units as shown in Figure 1.

Figure 1
Sew Four-Patch units as shown.

3. Sew two F triangles to an E piece as shown in Figure 2. Repeat for four units.

Figure 2
Sew units as shown.

4. Sew a C and CR to each D piece as shown in Figure 3.

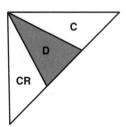

Figure 3
Sew units as shown.

5. Sew two Four-Patch units made in step 2 to one unit made in step 3 as shown in Figure 4.

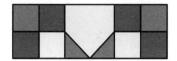

Figure 4
Sew units as shown.

6. Sew remaining two units made in step 3 to two sides of H as shown in Figure 5. Sew strips together as shown in Figure 6.

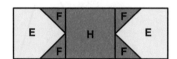

Figure 5
Sew unit as shown.

Figure 6
Sew strips together as shown.

7. Sew the triangles made in step 4 to each side of square as shown in block drawing.

8. Using squares cut from A template, sew four Four-Patch units as shown in Figure 7.

Figure 7
Sew Four-Patch units as shown.

9. Sew two border strips cut in step 1 to two opposite sides of block. Sew a Four-Patch unit made in step 8 to each end of remaining border strips referring to the Placement Diagram, sew strips to top and bottom of block.

Four-Patch Christmas Star
Placement Diagram
12" x 12"

10. Prepare for quilting as shown in General Instructions. Quilt as desired by hand or machine.

11. From holly print fabric, cut and piece enough 1½"-wide strips to make 1½ yards of binding as shown in General Instructions. Bind candle mat to finish. ❖

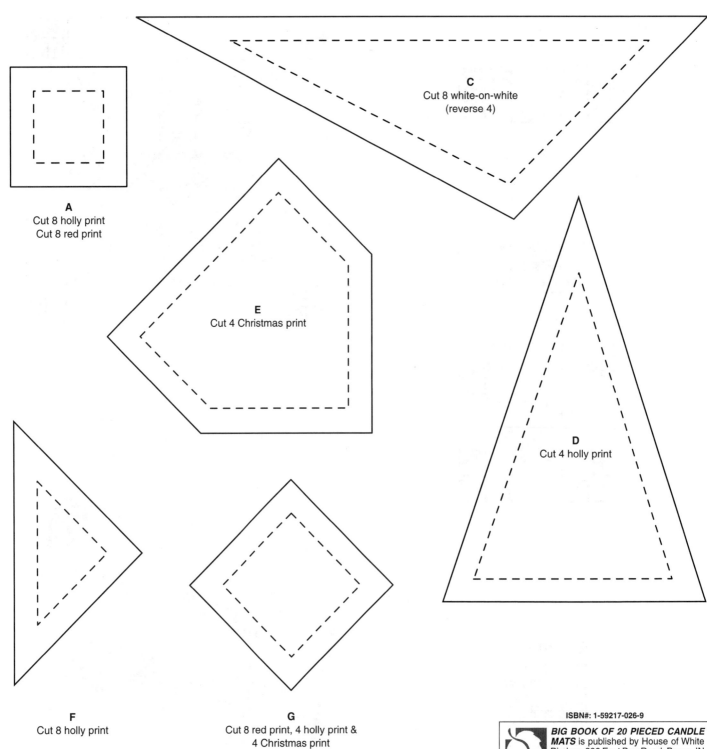

A
Cut 8 holly print
Cut 8 red print

C
Cut 8 white-on-white
(reverse 4)

E
Cut 4 Christmas print

D
Cut 4 holly print

F
Cut 8 holly print

G
Cut 8 red print, 4 holly print &
4 Christmas print

Our Keys to Success ...

Editor: Jeanne Stauffer; **Associate Editor**: Dianne Schmidt;
Technical Editor: Mary Jo Kurten; **Technical Artist**: Chad Summers;
Copy Editors: Michelle Beck, Nicki Lehman; **Graphic Arts Supervisor**:
Ronda Bechinski; **Graphic Artist**: Edith Teegarden; **Photography**:
Kelly Heydinger; **Photo Stylist**: Tammy Nussbaum

2 3 4 5 6 7 8 9

ISBN#: 1-59217-026-9

BIG BOOK OF 20 PIECED CANDLE MATS is published by House of White Birches, 306 East Parr Road, Berne, IN 46711, telephone (219) 589-4000. Printed in USA. Copyright © 2003 House of White Birches.

RETAILERS: If you would like to carry this pattern book or any other House of White Birches publications, call the Wholesale Department at Annie's Attic to set up a direct account: (903) 636-4303. Also, request a complete listing of publications available from House of White Birches.

Every effort has been made to ensure that the instructions in this pattern book are complete and accurate. We cannot, however, take responsibility for human error, typographical mistakes or variations in individual work.

E-mail: Customer_Service@whitebirches.com